BILL COSBY
Coming At You

by Sandra Ziegler
illustrated by Diana Magnuson

ELGIN, ILLINOIS 60120

We are grateful to the following companies for permission to use their photos.
Photos courtesy of UPI: pages 3, 15, 27, 28, 29, and 32.
Photo courtesy of the National Broadcasting Company, Inc.: page 25.

Library of Congress Cataloging in Publication Data

Ziegler, Sandra, 1938-
Bill Cosby, coming at you.

SUMMARY: A biographical sketch of the black comedian famous for anecdotes about his childhood.
1. Cosby, William H.—Juvenile literature.
2. Comedians—United States—Biography—Juvenile literature. [1. Cosby, William H. 2. Entertainers.
3. Afro-Americans—Biography] I. Magnuson, Diana.
II. Title.
PN2287.C632Z5 790.2′092′4 [B] [92] 78-9577
ISBN 0-89565-031-2

Distributed by Childrens Press, 1224 West Van Buren Street, Chicago, Illinois 60607.

"Did the things you tell about really happen?" a child asks Bill Cosby.

"Yes," says Bill.

And it's true. A lot of funny things happened to Bill when he was growing up.

Baby William Henry Cosby, Jr., arrived one July 12th. But Bill did not stay a baby long. He was bright and strong. At eight and one-half months old, he started not only to walk, but to run.

Bill Cosby was off on a wonderful adventure—his childhood.

Bill learned fast. When he was three or four, Bill learned how to get his mother to give him a cookie. Here is what he says.

"You know she'll say 'no' the first time you ask, but you know that if you can get her to laughing, you can get around her."

Bill went to kindergarten at Reynolds Elementary School. This was in North Philadelphia, Pennsylvania.

"Kindergarten," says Bill Cosby, "teaches you how to say good-by to your parents without crying."

Bill lived in a black ghetto. He did not have many things. But there was one thing he was never without, and that was stories. His mother, Anna Cosby, loved stories. She taught Bill to love them too. At bedtime, she often read to her boys until they dropped off to sleep.

"Some of my childhood was sad," Bill says. "But I don't like to talk about it. I like to think about the groovy things we did."

When Bill was eight years old, his brother James died. Then Bill's father went to work on a ship.

When Bill was nine, he became the man of the house. At that time, he and his family lived in an apartment in a North Philadelphia housing project.

Bill's mother had to work, so Bill became a part-time parent to his little brothers. He cooked them all of his favorite foods—spaghetti and meatballs, popcorn, and waffles. He colored the waffles

green,
purple,
orange, or
red.

When his brothers took naps, Bill Cosby ran out to play baseball in the street. He peeked in the window now and then just to be sure his brothers were all right.

Bill tells about playing other games, too, including basketball and football. He and his friends made their own rules to fit the city streets where they played.

Here is one of the football plays Bill tells his audiences about. "Someone in the gang says, 'Cosby, you go down to Third Street . . . catch the J bus . . . have him open the doors at 19th Street . . . and I'll fake her to ya.' "

Yes, Fat Albert, Dumb Donald, Weird Harold, Bowlegs, Junebug, the three Cosby kids—Bill, Bob, and Russell—the whole gang did have fun!

Many things happen to Fat Albert and the gang on TV. Most of them are things Bill Cosby remembers from his childhood. Of course, as he thinks and talks about them, he makes them funnier and funnier. So they are not exactly as they happened.

Though Bill spent lots of time playing, he did do other things. He was not very old when he made a shoeshine box out of wooden crates. Then he bought some shoe polish and washcloths. He went downtown to shine shoes. As he worked, he made people laugh.

When he made two dollars, Bill quit for that day. Sometimes, he kept a quarter for himself. But he gave most of the money to his mom.

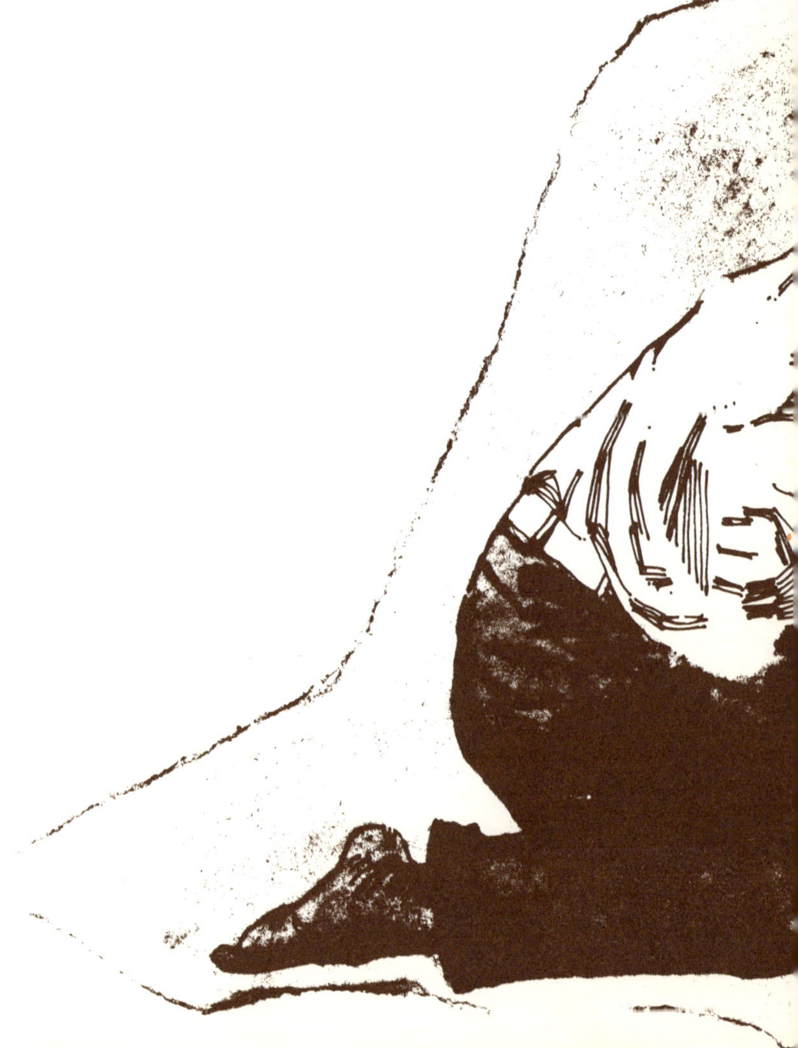

Bill had a favorite schoolteacher, Mary Nagle. Once she caught him telling a friend a joke. She had him tell the joke to the entire class. Then she asked him to tell jokes to the entire school at an assembly.

Mrs. Nagle also picked Bill to be the star in the class play. Perhaps she gave him his first real audience.

But even Mrs. Nagle couldn't make Bill Cosby see that life is more than just having fun.

"Bill Cosby would rather be a clown than a student," she said in a note to his mother.

Bill says, "It's just that I wanted to play."

After two years in the tenth grade, Bill quit school. Finally, he joined the Navy.

Good things happened to Bill Cosby after that. He began to grow up. While in the Navy, he got a high school diploma. When he came out, he went to college. There he was on the track team.

He also played football at college. He even thought of becoming a professional football player.

Bill jokes about playing football. "You go through the middle," he says. "You go through the guard slots. Every time . . . PHBAMMM!"

Maybe that's why he decided to become a comic instead. People didn't bang into him when he told stories. They listened, and they laughed, and they said, "Yeah . . . it was that way with me, too. PHBAMMM! Every time!"

Bill Cosby married Camille when he was just starting out as a performer. At first, they were poor. But, soon, Bill Cosby was doing well. People did like his stories. They laughed and laughed.

People laughed when Fat Albert said, "Hey, hey hey!" And they laughed when Noah said, "Right!" to God. One time, two times, three times, four times . . . Noah said, "Right!" to God. People laughed harder each time. And when God, in that deep voice, said, "Right!" right back to Noah, people laughed and laughed and laughed.

Before long, everyone wanted to hear Bill tell his funny stories. He became a star. He was the first black man to co-star in a television show that was on every week. The show was *I Spy.* Bill played a spy, a very smart spy, who spoke seven languages.

Bill Cosby and Robert Culp, of *I Spy*.

Bill Cosby now has five children. Their names are Erika, Erinn, Ennis, Erisa, and Evin. They keep him busy.

Since *I Spy,* other things have kept Bill busy too. He starred in another TV series, *The Bill Cosby Show.* In this one, he played a high school teacher and coach.

He made some movies. He wrote a book. He kept doing his comedy routines in night clubs and on TV.

Bill Cosby and Dick Van Dyke.

But Bill Cosby will tell you that some of his best work has been with the *Fat Albert* shows and with the *Electric Company*.

Bill Cosby with some children on the set of the *Electric Company*.

Preparing props for use on the *Electric Company*.
Can you tell what is missing from the sign?

Besides all these things, Bill Cosby went back to school. He went to classes, read books, and wrote papers.

One of his important school papers was about Fat Albert. But this time, Bill wasn't trying to write something funny. This time, he wrote about using Fat Albert to teach children.

For Bill Cosby is also a teacher. He has taught in school classrooms. He teaches on his TV shows.

Bill Cosby believes in kids. "I have met some kids," he says, "seven and eight year old kids, who will be able to do much more than I can do. I don't want to be a stumbling block to them. So I accept them the way they are."

If you should tune in to one of the *Fat Albert* shows, you'll see Dr. Bill Cosby. And you'll hear him say, "Here's Bill Cosby, coming at you . . . and if you're not careful, you may learn something."